AF480650

YOUTHFUL VISIONS, ENDLESS POSSIBILITIES

THE JOURNEY OF YOUNG MINDS WITH BIG DREAMS AND BOLD ACTION

DR. MINAKSHI BANSAL

Made with ♥ on the Notion Press Platform
www.notionpress.com

Contents

Contents

Contents

Prayer

*"Om Bhadram Karnebhih Shrinuyama Devah
Bhadram Pashyemakshabhiryajatrah
Sthirairangais Tushtuvamsastanubhih
Vyashema Devahitam Yadayuh
Svasti Na Indro Vriddhashravah
Svasti Nah Pusha Vishwavedah
Svasti Nastarkshyo Arishtanemih
Svasti No Brihaspatir Dadhatu
Om Shantih Shantih Shantih"*

This mantra is a prayer for universal well-being, invoking the blessings of various deities for protection, health, and happiness. It emphasizes the importance of experiencing the auspicious through all senses and living a life aligned with divine purpose. The repetition of "Shantih" at the end signifies a deep desire for peace in the individual, the environment, and the universe at large. This mantra is often recited as a prayer for peace, prosperity, and the physical and spiritual well-being of all beings.

ᘖᘖᘖ

About The Author

Dr. Minakshi Bansal, born in the bustling metropolis of Delhi, India, has led a life steeped in artistry, scholarly pursuit, and an unwavering commitment to societal betterment. Following her marriage, she relocated to Ahmedabad, Gujarat, where she has since blossomed into a multifaceted beacon of inspiration for many. Dr. Minakshi is not only recognized as a gifted artist in the realm of Fine Arts but also as an esteemed author, a devoted social worker and a dedicated research scholar in Psychology. Her journey, marked by a profound dedication to elevating those around her, especially the downtrodden and underprivileged children of society, is a testament to her deep-seated belief in the transformative power of engagement and empathy.

From her earliest days, Minakshi was distinguished by an insatiable appetite for reading. Her literary universe was inhabited by characters and narratives that spanned ethical tales, motivational and inspirational stories, and the mythic parables imbued with life lessons. This voracious reading habit was not merely for personal edification but was driven by a desire to distill and disseminate the essence of these narratives to foster the development of students and peers alike. She was particularly captivated by the lives and teachings of historical figures and spiritual leaders such as Adi Shankaracharya, Swami Vivekananda, Dr. APJ Abdul Kalam, Mahamana Pandit Madan Mohan Malviya, Mahatma Gandhi, Sardar Vallabhai Patel, and Vinoba Bhave, among others. Their philosophies and life stories fueled her ambition to embody their ideals of resilience, selflessness, and relentless pursuit of knowledge.

Dr. Minakshi's academic and practical engagement with psychology has been equally noteworthy. As a research scholar, her focus has been on exploring the intricate tapestry of the human psyche, aiming to unlock the potential for psychological well-being and societal harmony. Her scholarly work is complemented by her active involvement in social work, where she employs her academic insights to make tangible differences in the lives of the underprivileged. Her endeavours in social work are characterized by an innovative approach that combines traditional wisdom with contemporary psychological practices to address the multifaceted challenges faced by these communities.

Her artistic talents, another facet of her diverse capabilities, are not merely a personal passion but also serve as a medium through which she communicates and connects with others. Her art, rich in symbolism and emotional depth, reflects her philosophical inquiries and social concerns, offering viewers a glimpse into the breadth of her intellect and the depth of her compassion.

In addition to her contributions to the arts and social sciences, Dr. Minakshi has embraced the healing arts of Pranic Healing, mastering the techniques developed by Master Choa Kok Sui. This practice, which focuses on the manipulation of Prana or life energy to heal the body and aura, has been both a personal journey of discovery and a means through which she extends her healing touch to others. Her proficiency in Pranic Healing is complemented by her advocacy and teaching of various forms of meditation aimed at rejuvenation, personal betterment, and the cultivation of harmony within individuals and communities alike.

Dr. Minakshi's life is a narrative of relentless pursuit, not just of personal achievement but of the upliftment and empowerment of society at large. Her diverse interests and talents—spanning the arts, literature, psychology, and the healing practices—converge on a singular path of service. She embodies the spirit of the luminaries who inspired her, channelling their legacy through her actions and teachings. Through her books, art, and social initiatives, she continues to inspire a new generation to embark on their own journeys of self-discovery, resilience, and altruism.

Her commitment to social betterment, particularly her focus on uplifting underprivileged children, reflects a deep understanding of the transformative potential of education and personal development. By integrating her knowledge of psychology, her artistic sensibilities, and her healing practices, Dr. Bansal has developed a holistic approach to social work that addresses both the immediate needs and the long-term well-being of the communities she serves.

As an author, Dr. Minakshi's writings offer a blend of inspirational insights, practical wisdom, and reflective contemplations drawn from her extensive reading and life experiences. Her books serve as a guide for those seeking to navigate the complexities of life with grace, resilience, and purpose. Through her narratives, she extends an invitation to her readers to explore the depths of their own potential and to contribute meaningfully to the collective well-being of society.

In Dr. Minakshi Bansal, we find a remarkable synthesis of the artist, the scholar, the healer, and the social activist. Her life's work stands as a beacon of hope and a source of inspiration for individuals seeking to make a difference in the world. Her story is a compelling reminder of the power of individual action, rooted in compassion and driven by a profound commitment to the betterment of humanity. Dr. Minakshi's legacy is not just in the tangible outcomes of her efforts but in the enduring spirit of inquiry, empathy, and service that she embodies.

ppp

Preface

In this preface, I wish to illuminate the profound essence and purpose that drove the creation of this book—a work rooted deeply in admiration and belief in the power of youth. As societies worldwide grapple with unprecedented challenges and transformations, the roles that young individuals are stepping into are not just noticeable; they are pivotal. The narratives encapsulated within these pages are a testament to the vibrancy, resilience, and ingenuity of the younger generations. Their stories are not mere chronicles of achievement but resonant echoes of a future being actively and passionately shaped by young minds.

From climate activism to technological innovation, from cultural shifts to global connectivity, the youth of today are not waiting in the wings; they are leading the charge, breaking barriers, and crafting a world that aligns more closely with the ideals of equity, sustainability, and unity. It is a privilege to witness and document this dynamic era of young leadership—an era where challenges are vast but the possibilities and the visions for solutions are boundless.

The inspiration to write this book came from numerous interactions with young individuals, each brimming with ideas and eager to make a substantive mark on the world. These interactions revealed a common thread—a shared desire among youth to leverage their knowledge, skills, and energies in ways that transcend traditional boundaries. Whether it's through art, science, advocacy, or entrepreneurship, the drive to initiate positive change is a palpable force among young people across the globe.

This book is structured to reflect various facets of how young people are influencing and reshaping our world. Each chapter delves into different themes, ranging from the deeply personal journeys of young innovators and creators to the broad societal impacts of their actions. The stories shared here shine a light on both the successes and the struggles, offering a holistic view of the path toward impactful change. These narratives underscore a critical message: the actions taken today by the youth are not just about immediate outcomes but are stepping stones toward long-term, sustainable transformation.

The process of compiling these stories was both enlightening and humbling. It involved extensive research, interviews, and a lot of listening. The young individuals featured in this book come from diverse backgrounds and cultures, yet their stories converge on common themes of hope, determination, and the desire to contribute to something greater than themselves. Their insights and reflections are presented with the hope that they will inspire others—regardless of age—to consider how they, too, can contribute to positive changes in their communities and beyond.

Moreover, this book addresses the crucial support systems that enable youth to thrive. It discusses the roles of education, technology, and mentorship in nurturing young potential and preparing them for the challenges of tomorrow. It also explores the various ways society can and must adapt to facilitate and amplify the contributions of its younger members.

As we look ahead, the certainty of more challenges looms large; however, so does the promise of innovative solutions and the relentless spirit of youth. The young minds of today are already redefining leadership, accountability, and collaboration. Their journeys remind us that change is not only possible but ongoing, and that the mantle of progress is already in capable hands.

To all who venture into the pages of this book, whether you are a young person looking to find reflections of your own aspirations or someone from an earlier generation seeking to understand and support the architects of tomorrow, this work is for you. It is a celebration of youthful potential and a call to action for every one of us to support and amplify the bold strides being made by the younger generations.

Through this book, I extend an invitation to all readers to engage with the stories and ideas presented and to consider how they, too, can be part of the vibrant tapestry of change being woven by the youth of our time. The journey of young minds is not just about witnessing change but being an integral part of it. Here's to discovering the endless possibilities that lie ahead and to supporting the young visionaries who dare to turn their bold dreams into reality.

Dr. Minakshi Bansal
Social Activist
Ahmedabad, Gujarat, Bharat

ppp

ONE

DREAMING BIG: THE START OF SOMETHING NEW

The concept of dreaming big serves as the cornerstone of ambition and achievement, particularly among the youth whose aspirations paint a vibrant picture of the future. The act of dreaming big is not just about setting lofty goals but also embracing the limitless possibilities that lie ahead. It is a dynamic blend of imagination and courage, allowing young minds to envision not just what is, but what could be.

Dreams begin in the nebulous regions of our minds—a mixture of fleeting thoughts, profound emotions, and glimpses of what might be. For the youth, these dreams are often uninhibited, bold, and vibrant. They look beyond the constraints of current reality and into a realm of possibilities. This daring vision is crucial because it lays the groundwork for what comes next: turning those dreams into tangible goals. This initial phase of dreaming big is characterized by an exploratory spirit where failure is seen not as a setback but as a part of the learning process.

As these young dreamers begin to articulate their visions, their ideas start taking a more concrete shape. The dreams of writing revolutionary software, inventing new eco-friendly materials, or even becoming an advocate for social change are nurtured by their environment and the encouragement they receive. Here, the role of educators, family members, and mentors is pivotal. Supportive relationships can significantly influence a young person's ability to believe in their dreams. Encouragement acts like the sun to these budding aspirations, providing the energy needed to grow and flourish.

Transforming Dreams into Defined Goals

However, dreaming is just the beginning. The true challenge lies in transforming these dreams into defined goals. This transformation requires self-awareness, discipline, and a willingness to take practical steps towards these ends. Young minds learn to set SMART goals—Specific, Measurable, Achievable, Relevant, and Time-bound—which provide a framework that transforms airy dreams into achievable objectives.

This process also involves a strategic assessment of what skills and resources are needed to reach these goals. Whether it's pursuing advanced education, seeking out mentorship, or gaining real-world experience through internships or volunteering, each step is a calculated move towards achieving their dreams.

One of the most empowering aspects of dreaming big is the development of a proactive mindset. Youth who engage in this practice learn not to wait for opportunities to come to their doorstep but to go out and create them.

They become initiators, driven by their goals and the knowledge that they have the power to make things happen. This proactive approach is seen in young entrepreneurs who start their businesses, young activists who organize community movements, and young artists who carve out their own niches in competitive industries.

Overcoming Challenges and Staying Inspired

Naturally, the path is not always smooth. Young dreamers face numerous challenges—financial limitations, lack of guidance, societal pressures, or even self-doubt. However, it's their ability to persevere through these obstacles that often determines their success. Resilience becomes a critical skill, as does the ability to adapt and pivot when necessary.

The stories of successful young individuals rarely follow a straight line; they are filled with detours and lessons learned along the way.

Moreover, staying inspired can sometimes be as challenging as confronting physical obstacles. Keeping the flame of ambition alive requires continual motivation and often, a return to the original source of inspiration. Many successful young people keep their dreams vivid in their minds by visualizing their goals regularly, reaffirming their commitment, and celebrating small victories along the way.

As young individuals make headway towards their dreams, they also begin to inspire others. Their journeys become a beacon for their peers, demonstrating that young people can drive significant change and that their contributions are invaluable. This collective momentum can transform communities and create a new culture of achievement and innovation.

The journey from dreaming to achieving is full of challenges and opportunities. It requires courage, resilience, and support, but most importantly, it begins with the freedom to dream big. By fostering environments where young people are encouraged to dream and equipped to turn those dreams into reality, society can unlock a powerful source of progress and innovation.

The energy and creativity of young minds are one of the greatest assets available to the world, and by nurturing these qualities, we can expect a future that is as vibrant and promising as the dreams that shape it.

ᐅᐅᐅ

"In the hands of the youth, technology becomes more than a tool; it becomes a beacon of hope and a blueprint for a sustainable future. Their innovations are the threads weaving a tapestry of change, proving that when technology meets compassion, the world shifts."

ᗑᗑᗑ

TWO

THE POWER OF CURIOSITY: EXPLORING THE WORLD AROUND US

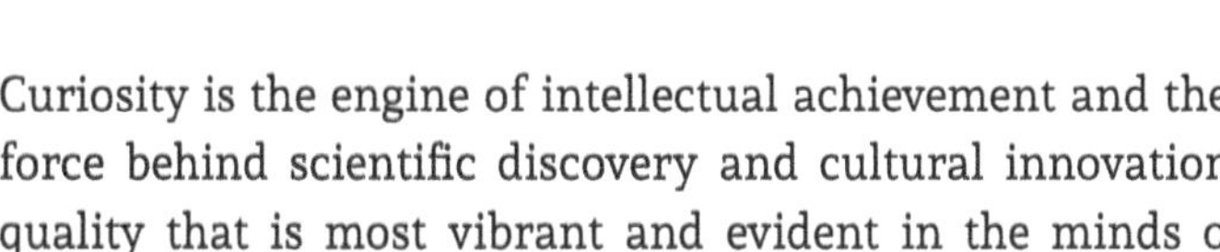

Curiosity is the engine of intellectual achievement and the driving force behind scientific discovery and cultural innovation. It is a quality that is most vibrant and evident in the minds of young individuals. This innate desire to know more about the world, to understand how things work, and to explore unknown territories, is what propels the youth toward learning and discovery. Curiosity does not only lead to the acquisition of knowledge; it also fosters empathy and understanding across cultural divides, making it a crucial trait for the global leaders of tomorrow.

At its core, curiosity prompts the question "Why?" This simple question can unravel the most complex mysteries of science, can lead to the development of new technologies, and can deepen our understanding of human behavior and societal structures. For young people, this quest begins with an observation of their immediate environment and gradually expands to include wider, more complex systems and ideas. It leads them to read books, participate in experiments, and engage with diverse cultures, allowing them to gain a broader perspective of the world.

Cultivating Curiosity in Educational Settings

Education systems play a critical role in either nurturing or stifling curiosity. Traditional education methods often prioritize rote learning and standardized testing, which can suppress curiosity and discourage creative thinking. However, progressive educational models that encourage inquiry-based learning can help foster a culture of curiosity. These models advocate for student-led learning where young individuals are encouraged to pursue their interests, ask questions, and explore topics deeply. This approach not only makes learning more enjoyable but also more meaningful, as students connect their studies to real-world contexts.

Furthermore, the role of educators is pivotal in cultivating curiosity. Teachers who pose challenging questions and encourage open-ended exploration inspire students to think critically and independently. By creating a classroom environment that welcomes mistakes as learning opportunities, educators can help students overcome the fear of the unknown and embrace the process of discovery. This support is vital in helping young minds understand that the pursuit of knowledge is an ongoing and often non-linear journey.

Technology and Curiosity

In today's digital age, technology offers unprecedented opportunities to satisfy curiosity. The internet, for example, is a vast repository of information where young minds can find answers to almost any question within seconds. However, the real power of technology is not just in delivering information but in enabling connections between ideas, disciplines, and cultures. Platforms that encourage collaboration and sharing of ideas can enhance creativity and innovation, allowing young individuals to learn from and with others around the globe.

Yet, with the vast resources available, there is a challenge in teaching young people to navigate this information responsibly and critically. Learning how to discern credible sources, understanding the basis of arguments, and evaluating evidence are all crucial skills in using technology to satisfy curiosity effectively. As young individuals learn to use these digital tools responsibly, they enhance their ability to use curiosity as a lever for learning and personal growth.

Curiosity Beyond Academics

Curiosity also extends beyond academic pursuits—it plays a crucial role in personal development. It drives young individuals to explore their identities, understand their emotions, and navigate their relationships. This introspective curiosity is essential for developing emotional intelligence and resilience. Additionally, curiosity drives young people to engage with diverse cultures, languages, and traditions, which fosters global understanding and cooperation.

Moreover, curiosity can manifest as a desire to change prevailing conditions, leading to social innovation and entrepreneurship. Young individuals, driven by curiosity about societal issues, can develop new solutions to age-old problems. Their fresh perspectives and boundless energy can lead to social movements that challenge the status quo and drive societal progress.

The power of curiosity lies in its ability to open doors to new knowledge, new experiences, and new connections. It is both a personal trait and a societal asset, leading to discoveries that propel human progress. By nurturing curiosity in young people, we prepare them not only to adapt to the changes of the future but also to lead those changes. Encouraging a curious mindset in the next generation is essential for fostering a culture that values learning, innovation, and understanding—qualities that are crucial for the complex, interconnected world they are about to inherit.

ᐅᐅᐅ

"Young minds are not just preparing for the future;
they are actively sculpting it with every bold step
and innovative idea. Their dreams are blueprints
for a world reimagined, where diversity and
inclusion form the foundation of every community."

🖤🖤🖤

THREE

FROM PASSION TO ACTION: MAKING IDEAS HAPPEN

The journey from harboring a passion to taking action is one that defines the trajectory of many young visionaries. Passion is the intense emotion that ignites the spark of creativity and drives individuals to go beyond mere thinking into doing. It is the fuel for persistence in the face of adversity and the source of inspiration when paths seem unclear. But how do young people transform this raw energy into tangible outcomes? This transformation is not merely about having strong feelings towards a cause or an idea; it's about channeling these feelings to create, innovate, and implement solutions that have a real impact.

The first step in turning passion into action is defining a clear vision. This involves understanding what you are passionate about and why it matters. It requires introspection and a deep dive into the values that drive this passion. For many young individuals, this might mean identifying issues they feel strongly about, such as climate change, education reform, or technological innovation, and envisioning what changes they would like to see. This vision sets the groundwork for all subsequent actions and serves as a constant reminder of what they are working towards.

Setting Goals and Creating a Roadmap

Once the vision is clear, the next step is to set practical goals. These goals act as milestones that guide the journey from concept to reality. Goal setting involves breaking down the vision into actionable steps. This could mean starting a social enterprise, launching a community project, or developing a new app. Each goal should be specific, measurable, achievable, relevant, and time-bound (SMART). This framework ensures that goals are within reach and align with the larger vision.

Creating a roadmap involves planning the steps needed to achieve these goals. This might include conducting research, acquiring necessary skills, securing funding, or building a team. The roadmap not only provides a structured approach to achieving goals but also helps anticipate potential challenges and plan for contingencies.

Mobilizing Resources

Turning passion into action requires more than just a well-laid plan; it necessitates mobilizing resources. This includes gathering the physical, financial, and human resources necessary to bring ideas to life. Young innovators often start by tapping into their networks to find mentors, collaborators, and supporters who share their vision. They might also look for funding opportunities through grants, crowdfunding, or angel investors.

Technology plays a crucial role in mobilizing resources by providing platforms for collaboration, fundraising, and marketing. Social media, for example, can be a powerful tool to raise awareness, build communities around a cause, and engage with stakeholders. It also provides a platform for transparency, allowing others to see the progress of a project, which can help gain further support and traction.

Overcoming Obstacles

The path from passion to action is rarely smooth. Young individuals often face numerous challenges, from bureaucratic hurdles and financial constraints to skepticism from peers and society. Overcoming these obstacles requires resilience, adaptability, and a problem-solving mindset. It's important for young leaders to remain committed to their vision but flexible in their approach. They need to be willing to learn from failures and view obstacles as opportunities to grow and innovate.

Additionally, developing a support network can provide a critical safety net. Having mentors, peers, or even role models who have navigated similar paths can offer guidance, encouragement, and practical advice. These relationships not only help overcome current challenges but also pave the way for future opportunities.

Building Momentum and Making an Impact

As projects begin to take shape and initial goals are met, it is important to maintain momentum. This can be achieved by continuously setting new goals, scaling impacts, and finding new avenues to apply passion. Success breeds more success, and as young innovators begin to see the results of their work, it fuels further innovation and dedication.

Furthermore, making a real impact requires reflection and responsiveness to feedback. It involves measuring the outcomes of actions taken and being open to making adjustments. This continuous loop of action, feedback, and adaptation helps refine the approach and outcomes, ensuring that the impact is meaningful and sustainable.

Ttransforming passion into action is a dynamic process that requires clarity of vision, meticulous planning, mobilization of resources, resilience in the face of challenges, and a commitment to continuous improvement. For young individuals driven by a desire to make a difference, the journey from passion to action is not just about achieving personal goals but about contributing to a larger cause and making a lasting impact in the world.

ᐅᐅᐅ

"Art and activism converge in the melody of youth,
where every note sung and every stroke painted
tells a story of change. These are the anthems of a
new era, echoing far beyond the confines of galleries
and concert halls."

♥♥♥

FOUR

BREAKING BARRIERS: OVERCOMING OBSTACLES ON THE PATH TO SUCCESS

The path to success is rarely a straight line. It is often filled with obstacles that can challenge the spirit, test resolve, and require perseverance. For young individuals, especially those just starting their journey, these barriers can seem daunting. However, overcoming these challenges is not just about reaching a destination but about growing and becoming more resilient along the way. The ability to confront and navigate these obstacles effectively is a crucial skill for anyone seeking to make a significant impact in their field or community.

Obstacles can come in various forms—be it societal norms, financial constraints, personal limitations, or institutional barriers. Each type of obstacle presents unique challenges and requires specific strategies to overcome. Understanding these challenges and adopting a problem-solving mindset is the first step towards turning barriers into stepping stones.

Identifying and Understanding Barriers

The first crucial step in overcoming obstacles is to clearly identify and understand them. This involves a deep dive into the nature of the barriers, their origins, and the ways in which they affect progress. For young people, this might mean acknowledging societal expectations that dictate certain career paths over others, recognizing biases that might exist within their chosen fields, or facing the economic realities that limit their opportunities.

Once these barriers are identified, the next step is to seek out resources, knowledge, and skills that can help in overcoming them. This might involve seeking mentorship, pursuing educational opportunities, or connecting with others who have faced similar challenges. Understanding the barriers also involves a self-assessment of one's strengths and weaknesses. This self-awareness allows individuals to craft a personalized approach to overcoming obstacles, utilizing their strengths to their advantage, and working on areas where they are less robust.

Cultivating Resilience and Adaptability

Resilience is perhaps the most critical trait for anyone facing significant barriers. It is the ability to bounce back from setbacks and to continue pursuing one's goals despite difficulties. Cultivating resilience involves developing a positive mindset, one that views challenges as opportunities to learn and grow rather than insurmountable problems. It also involves building a strong support network that can provide emotional backing and practical advice.

Adaptability goes hand in hand with resilience. It is the ability to adjust one's strategies and approaches in response to changing circumstances. For young individuals, being adaptable might mean revising their goals, exploring alternate paths, or even shifting focus when necessary. The key is to remain committed to the overarching vision while being flexible in how to achieve it.

Leveraging Support Networks

No one overcomes significant obstacles alone. Building and leveraging a support network is crucial for success. This network can include family, friends, mentors, and professional contacts. Each of these relationships provides different forms of support—emotional, informational, and practical. For instance, mentors can offer guidance based on their experiences, friends can provide emotional support, and professional contacts can open doors to new opportunities.

In addition to personal networks, many young people benefit from joining or forming communities with those who share similar goals or have faced similar barriers. These communities can provide a platform for sharing resources, offering encouragement, and collaborating on solutions to common challenges. In the digital age, these communities can be both local and global, allowing young individuals to connect with a diverse range of people and ideas.

Implementing Practical Strategies

Once the barriers are understood, resilience is fostered, and support networks are established, the next step is to implement practical strategies to overcome these obstacles. This could involve developing specific skills, applying for scholarships or grants, launching awareness campaigns, or starting a business. Each strategy should be tailored to the specific barrier and designed with the individual's strengths and resources in mind.

For example, if financial constraints are a barrier, strategies might include crowdfunding for a project, applying for financial aid, or starting a part-time business. If societal norms pose a challenge, efforts might focus on advocacy and public awareness to shift these perceptions.

Overcoming obstacles on the path to success is an integral part of personal and professional development. It requires understanding the nature of the barriers, cultivating resilience, leveraging support networks, and implementing practical strategies. By approaching challenges with a problem-solving mindset and viewing them as opportunities for growth, young individuals can not only achieve their goals but also strengthen their capacity to face future challenges. This journey, though fraught with hurdles, is immensely rewarding and a critical component of building a fulfilling and impactful career.

ᐇᐇᐇ

"Through the lens of youthful vision, challenges transform into stepping stones towards monumental change. Each setback, a lesson learned; every failure, a cornerstone for resilience."

ᐳᐳᐳ

FIVE

THE SPIRIT OF INNOVATION: YOUNG INVENTORS AND THEIR CREATIONS

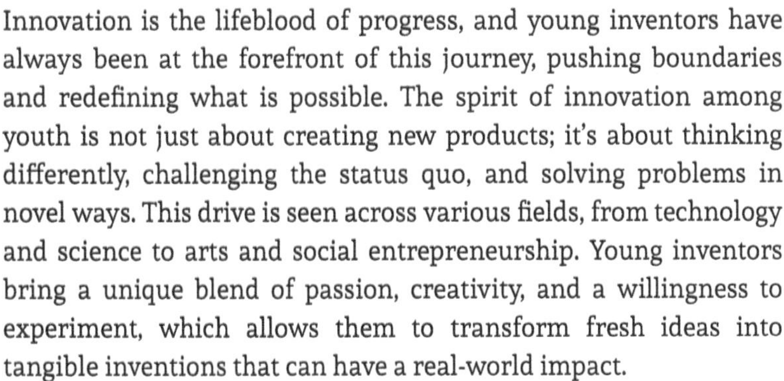

Innovation is the lifeblood of progress, and young inventors have always been at the forefront of this journey, pushing boundaries and redefining what is possible. The spirit of innovation among youth is not just about creating new products; it's about thinking differently, challenging the status quo, and solving problems in novel ways. This drive is seen across various fields, from technology and science to arts and social entrepreneurship. Young inventors bring a unique blend of passion, creativity, and a willingness to experiment, which allows them to transform fresh ideas into tangible inventions that can have a real-world impact.

The journey of young inventors often begins with a simple spark—a moment of curiosity, a problem that no one has solved, or a daily inconvenience that could be improved. From this initial spark, a powerful process of exploration, experimentation, and execution unfolds, potentially leading to groundbreaking innovations.

Cultivating a Culture of Creativity and Experimentation

Creating an environment that nurtures creativity and encourages experimentation is crucial for fostering innovation. Educational institutions, communities, and families play a pivotal role in this by providing the necessary resources and support. Schools that offer labs, maker spaces, and innovation hubs give students the physical space to experiment and build. Meanwhile, competitions, hackathons, and science fairs provide not only motivation but also a platform for young innovators to showcase their work and receive feedback.

Furthermore, it's essential to encourage a mindset that views failures as stepping stones rather than roadblocks. This perspective is vital for young inventors, as the path of innovation is fraught with challenges and setbacks. Learning to pivot, iterate, and persevere through difficulties is part of what shapes a successful inventor.

Harnessing Technology and Collaboration

In today's digital age, technology provides tools that can significantly amplify the impact of young inventors. Access to information, advanced software, and connectivity with global networks has democratized the process of invention. Young innovators can now conduct research, learn from top experts in the field, and collaborate with peers from around the world, all from their own homes or local libraries.

Collaboration is particularly powerful, as it combines diverse perspectives and skills, often leading to more innovative and comprehensive solutions. Platforms that facilitate collaboration, such as social media groups, online forums, and virtual workshops, enable young inventors to exchange ideas, critique each other's work, and improve upon existing designs.

Stories of Young Inventors

The stories of young inventors are as diverse as they are inspiring. Consider the example of a teenager who invented a new method of purifying water using renewable energy sources, addressing both environmental sustainability and access to clean water. Another young innovator developed a smartphone app that uses artificial intelligence to help people with visual impairments navigate their surroundings. These stories highlight how young minds are not only capable of complex problem-solving but are also deeply committed to making a positive impact on society.

These young inventors often start with a personal passion or a challenge they observe in their community. Their inventions are not just about technical skill; they reflect a deep understanding of the needs and challenges facing today's world. They think beyond traditional methods and are not afraid to disrupt established industries with their fresh, bold ideas.

Impact on Society and the Economy

The contributions of young inventors extend far beyond the immediate applications of their inventions. By introducing new products, services, and methods, they stimulate economic activity and often create new markets and jobs. Furthermore, their work inspires other young people to pursue their curiosity and creativity, leading to a virtuous cycle of innovation.

Additionally, these young minds often bring a new level of attention to critical issues such as sustainability, accessibility, and health. Through their inventions, they not only offer solutions but also raise awareness and prompt action from older generations, policymakers, and business leaders.

In conclusion, the spirit of innovation in young inventors is a powerful force for change. By transforming original ideas into practical solutions, these young minds play a crucial role in driving progress across all sectors of society. Their journey from ideation to creation is filled with challenges, but it is their unique perspective, relentless pursuit of knowledge, and unwavering determination that enable them to leave a lasting impact on the world. The future looks bright, illuminated by the brilliance of young inventors and their creations, which continue to push the boundaries of what is possible.

"The digital landscape is vast, but young navigators are charting courses that lead to unexplored territories of impact and inclusivity. Their journey is a testament to the power of connected minds in creating waves of positive change."

ᐯᐯᐯ

SIX

BUILDING BRIDGES: YOUNG LEADERS IN COMMUNITY ENGAGEMENT

Community engagement is essential for fostering a connected, resilient, and vibrant society. Young leaders play a pivotal role in this realm, bringing fresh perspectives, energy, and a unique ability to bridge various segments of the community. Their involvement often leads to innovative solutions to local issues, creating a positive impact that resonates well beyond their immediate environment. Young leaders in community engagement not only help address pressing local needs but also build a foundation for long-term civic involvement and leadership.

The journey of young community leaders often starts with a deep sense of empathy and a commitment to service. Motivated by a desire to contribute to their communities, these young individuals step forward to lead initiatives that bring people together, advocate for social justice, and provide resources and support where they are most needed.

Empathy and Action: The Core of Community Leadership

At the heart of effective community leadership lies empathy—the ability to understand and share the feelings of others. Young leaders are particularly adept at this, as they often share similar experiences with their peers and can relate to the challenges faced by other age groups through family and community ties. This empathy drives them to take action and advocate for others, pushing for changes that benefit not just individuals but the entire community.

Empathy also fosters a sense of belonging and solidarity, crucial for any community project. When leaders show genuine concern and commitment, it inspires trust and encourages more community members to get involved. This collaborative approach is vital for the sustainability of community initiatives, ensuring that they are more than just one-off projects but part of a continuous effort to improve the community.

Harnessing Technology and Social Media

Young leaders are often at the forefront of using technology and social media to enhance community engagement. These tools enable them to reach a wider audience, gather support, and mobilize resources more efficiently. Social media platforms, in particular, provide a powerful medium for raising awareness about issues, sharing success stories, and calling for action. They allow young leaders to connect with community members, local businesses, and government officials, facilitating a more integrated approach to community development.

Moreover, technology enables the collection and analysis of data to identify needs, track progress, and measure the impact of community projects. This data-driven approach ensures that efforts are targeted and effective, addressing the most pressing issues and adapting to changing circumstances.

Initiatives and Impact

Young leaders often initiate projects that address a variety of community needs. These can range from environmental conservation efforts, such as organizing community clean-ups and promoting recycling, to social welfare initiatives like food drives, educational programs, and health awareness campaigns. Each initiative not only addresses specific issues but also helps foster a culture of participation and responsibility.

For example, young leaders might organize workshops that educate community members about sustainable practices or health issues. They might also set up mentorship programs that connect professionals with youth to foster career development and skills acquisition. Through these activities, young leaders not only provide valuable services but also strengthen the social fabric of their communities.

Overcoming Challenges

Despite their enthusiasm and commitment, young community leaders often face significant challenges. These can include limited resources, lack of experience, and sometimes skepticism from older community members. Overcoming these challenges requires persistence, creativity, and a willingness to learn and adapt.

Building partnerships with established organizations can provide young leaders with the support and resources they need. These partnerships can offer mentorship, funding, and access to networks that can help amplify their efforts. Additionally, by demonstrating transparency, accountability, and tangible results, young leaders can build credibility and trust within the community, ensuring continued support for their initiatives.

Empowering Others

One of the most significant impacts of young leaders in community engagement is their ability to empower others. By involving peers in their projects, they not only expand their impact but also inspire a new generation of community-minded individuals. This empowerment creates a ripple effect, as more people become engaged and take on leadership roles within the community.

Young leaders in community engagement play a crucial role in building bridges between diverse groups and addressing community needs. Their unique blend of empathy, technological savvy, and innovative thinking enables them to lead effective initiatives that strengthen community ties and enhance the quality of life for all members. As they overcome challenges and empower others, they lay the groundwork for a more connected, engaged, and resilient society, demonstrating the profound impact that dedicated, compassionate leadership can have on the world.

ϷϷϷ

"In the echo of young voices, the sound of revolution finds its rhythm. They speak not just to express but to challenge and reshape the world around them, turning whispers of change into roars of progress."

♥♥♥

SEVEN

THE DIGITAL FRONTIER: YOUTH TRANSFORMING TECHNOLOGY

In the rapidly evolving landscape of technology, young individuals stand at the forefront, driving change and innovation. This generation of digital natives, having grown up with the internet, smartphones, and social media, is uniquely equipped to leverage technology in ways that transform not just how we interact with digital tools, but how we live, learn, and connect with each other. Their intrinsic understanding of and familiarity with digital environments enable them to create and adapt technologies that push the boundaries of what is possible.

The influence of youth in the realm of technology can be seen in various areas including software development, hardware innovation, digital media, and e-commerce. They are not only consumers of technology but also increasingly its creators, shaping the digital landscape with their fresh perspectives and visionary ideas.

Pioneering New Technologies

Young tech innovators have been responsible for some of the most groundbreaking developments in recent years. From new apps that solve everyday problems to sophisticated algorithms that power artificial intelligence, the contributions of young minds have been crucial. Their projects often start as simple ideas developed in school projects, hackathons, or even in their bedrooms, and can evolve into products and services used by millions around the globe.

The ability to see technology through a lens unclouded by the constraints of traditional methods and practices allows these young pioneers to think differently. For instance, many youth-led initiatives focus on using technology to address social and environmental issues, such as developing apps that promote recycling or platforms that facilitate access to education for underprivileged children. These efforts highlight how technology can be a powerful tool for good, addressing significant societal challenges.

Leveraging the Power of Networks

One of the key advantages that young people have today is the ability to connect and collaborate across borders. The internet has democratized access to information and expertise, allowing young innovators to learn from the best, find mentors, and collaborate on projects with peers from around the world. Online forums, social media platforms, and virtual learning communities serve as hubs where ideas are exchanged, and partnerships are formed.

Moreover, crowdfunding platforms have opened new avenues for acquiring funding, enabling young tech entrepreneurs to bypass traditional barriers to entry such as the need for venture capital or large initial investments. By presenting their ideas directly to potential users and supporters, young innovators can secure the resources needed to develop and test their technologies.

Impact on Industries

The impact of young tech innovators is not confined to the tech industry alone; it extends across all sectors including healthcare, education, agriculture, and finance. For example, young developers have created apps that allow farmers to monitor crop health remotely, or platforms that provide real-time medical data to patients and doctors to improve the quality of care. In education, we see a surge in technologies aimed at enhancing learning through interactive and personalized digital platforms.

These technologies often disrupt existing models, challenging traditional businesses and institutions to adapt or innovate. The push from these young minds leads to industries becoming more agile, more innovative, and often, more inclusive.

Challenges and Opportunities

While the opportunities are vast, young innovators face significant challenges. Technical and regulatory hurdles, intellectual property issues, and the digital divide are just some of the obstacles that can impede progress. Moreover, there is often a gap between having a revolutionary idea and having the business acumen to bring it to market effectively.

Education systems that support STEM (science, technology, engineering, and mathematics) education, combined with business training, can prepare young tech innovators better for the challenges they will face. Furthermore, policies that support open data, protect privacy, and ensure fair competition are crucial for nurturing an environment where young tech entrepreneurs can thrive.

The role of youth in transforming technology is pivotal. With their deep understanding of digital technologies and their potential, young innovators are not only shaping the future of technology but also the future of society. They bring a fresh perspective that often challenges conventional wisdom and drives innovation at a pace that was unimaginable just a few decades ago. As they continue to break barriers and create new possibilities, the digital frontier is ever-expanding, promising a future that is increasingly interconnected and empowered by technology.

"As young leaders forge paths in uncharted territories, their footsteps leave imprints for future generations to follow. Their leadership is a blend of innovation and wisdom beyond their years, lighting up paths in the darkest of times."

EIGHT

ART AND THE YOUNG MIND: CREATIVITY AS A CATALYST FOR CHANGE

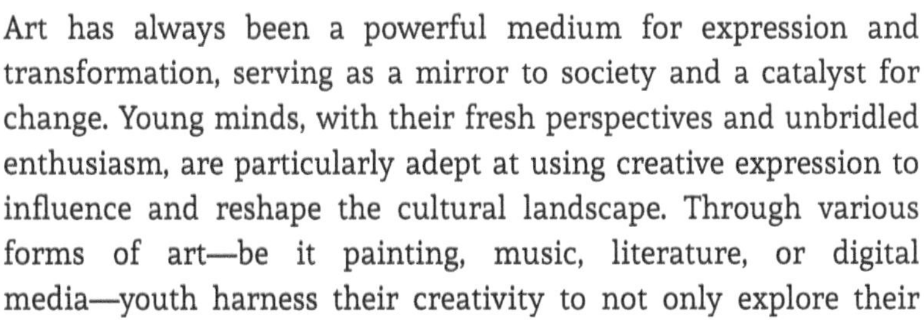

Art has always been a powerful medium for expression and transformation, serving as a mirror to society and a catalyst for change. Young minds, with their fresh perspectives and unbridled enthusiasm, are particularly adept at using creative expression to influence and reshape the cultural landscape. Through various forms of art—be it painting, music, literature, or digital media—youth harness their creativity to not only explore their identities but also to address and challenge societal issues.

The connection between creativity and innovation is evident in how young artists approach their crafts. They are often at the vanguard of cultural shifts, using their artworks to provoke thought, stir emotions, and inspire action. This dynamic interaction between art and young creators is pivotal as it fosters a more engaged, empathetic, and proactive generation.

The Role of Art in Youth Development

Art plays a crucial role in the cognitive, emotional, and social development of young individuals. Creatively engaged youth tend to exhibit higher levels of empathy, self-awareness, and critical thinking. These qualities are essential for personal growth and for fostering a sense of connection with others. Artistic endeavors enable young creators to explore complex feelings and ideas in a constructive and often therapeutic way. This exploration is crucial during adolescence and young adulthood—a time of identity formation and self-discovery.

Moreover, the process of creating art can be as impactful as the final product. It teaches resilience and problem-solving, as young artists often have to navigate through challenges such as technical limitations, creative blocks, and critical feedback. These experiences build perseverance and adaptability, skills that are applicable beyond the artistic domain and into personal and professional life.

Art as a Social Commentary

Many young artists use their work as a form of social commentary, tackling issues such as inequality, environmental degradation, and human rights. By addressing these topics, they not only raise awareness but also foster dialogue and inspire others to reflect and act. Art becomes a vehicle for social change, engaging viewers and participants in deeper, more meaningful conversations about the world they live in.

In recent years, the accessibility of digital platforms has amplified the reach and impact of young artists. Social media, for instance, allows artworks to be shared widely and instantaneously, reaching diverse audiences across the globe. This democratization of art has given rise to new voices and has enabled young creators from marginalized communities to express themselves and gain visibility.

Collaborative Art and Community Engagement

Collaboration is a significant aspect of contemporary art, and young creators often engage in collaborative projects that enhance community ties and promote cultural exchange. These projects can take various forms, such as community murals, performance art, and digital media collaborations. Through these collective endeavors, artists not only pool their talents and resources but also learn from one another, enriching their own artistic practices.

Community-based art projects are particularly powerful in bringing people together and in catalyzing community development. They can transform public spaces, invigorate local cultures, and strengthen communal bonds. Moreover, such initiatives often provide young artists with opportunities to lead and manage projects, honing their organizational and leadership skills.

Innovation in Artistic Techniques and Media

The adventurous spirit of the youth drives innovation in artistic techniques and media. Young creators are often early adopters of new technologies, incorporating them into their art to push the boundaries of traditional forms. From digital illustration and animation to virtual reality and interactive installations, the integration of new technologies in art has opened up new avenues for creativity and interaction.

These technological advancements not only enhance the aesthetic qualities of art but also broaden the scope of its influence.

Interactive art, for example, engages the audience directly, making the experience more personal and impactful. Such innovations redefine the relationship between the artist, the artwork, and the audience, fostering a more active and immersive engagement with art.

Nurturing Creativity and Advocacy

Supporting and nurturing the creative talents of youth is crucial for the continued vitality of the arts and for ensuring that young voices remain central in cultural conversations. Educational systems, community organizations, and policy-makers play critical roles in providing young artists with the resources, platforms, and encouragement they need. Additionally, recognizing and celebrating young talent motivates aspiring artists to pursue their passions and use their creative skills for social good.

The intersection of art and the young mind is a fertile ground for creativity, innovation, and change. Through their artistic expressions, young creators not only enhance their personal development but also contribute to societal growth. Their art transcends aesthetic values, embodying hopes, challenges, and aspirations of a generation poised to reshape the cultural landscape. As they continue to break new ground, young artists reaffirm the transformative power of creativity, making it a profound catalyst for change.

ppp

"Young environmentalists are not just advocates for the earth; they are its fiercest protectors. Their actions today are the lifelines preserving tomorrow, ensuring that our planet's heartbeat continues to echo through the ages."

♡♡♡

NINE

GREEN DREAMS: YOUNG ENVIRONMENTAL ADVOCATES

In a world increasingly affected by climate change and environmental degradation, young environmental advocates stand at the forefront of the sustainability movement. These passionate individuals are not just concerned about the future; they are actively shaping it through innovative solutions, advocacy, and grassroots activism. Their green dreams encompass a vision of a planet where ecosystems thrive, resources are used responsibly, and sustainable practices are the norm, not the exception.

Young environmental advocates come from diverse backgrounds and each brings a unique perspective to the environmental movement. Their efforts are crucial in driving change at local, national, and global levels, and they utilize a range of strategies from policy advocacy to community education and technological innovation.

Understanding and Engaging with Environmental Issues

The journey of many young environmental advocates begins with education and awareness. By understanding the science behind environmental issues, such as climate change, biodiversity loss, and pollution, young advocates are better equipped to address these challenges. Schools, non-profit organizations, and community groups play vital roles in providing the necessary education that sparks interest and concern for the environment.

Once armed with knowledge, young advocates often engage in raising awareness about environmental issues within their communities. They organize workshops, create informative content for social media, and participate in or lead environmental campaigns. Their approach is often inclusive and collaborative, aiming to bring together individuals from various sectors of society to foster a broader understanding and commitment to environmental stewardship.

Grassroots Activism and Policy Advocacy

At the heart of the environmental movement led by youth is grassroots activism. This involves mobilizing community members to participate in environmental conservation activities such as tree planting, clean-up drives, and renewable energy projects. These activities not only contribute directly to environmental conservation but also help build a community culture that values and prioritizes sustainability.

Beyond local initiatives, young environmental advocates often engage in policy advocacy. Understanding that long-term sustainability requires systemic change, they strive to influence environmental policies at all levels of government. Through petitions, demonstrations, and participation in public forums, young advocates work to ensure that environmental considerations are integral to policy-making. Their efforts can lead to the implementation of stricter environmental regulations, the development of sustainable urban planning, and the adoption of green technologies.

Leveraging Technology for Environmental Sustainability

Technology plays a crucial role in modern environmental advocacy. Young environmentalists are particularly adept at using digital tools to enhance their advocacy efforts. Social media platforms allow them to reach a global audience, spread their message, and mobilize international support for environmental causes. They also use technology to monitor environmental changes, collect data, and develop solutions that help mitigate environmental impacts.

Innovative technologies such as GIS (Geographic Information Systems) and remote sensing are used by young advocates to track deforestation, monitor wildlife populations, and manage natural resources more efficiently. Additionally, young innovators are at the forefront of developing sustainable technologies such as biodegradable materials, renewable energy systems, and water purification technologies.

Collaboration and International Cooperation

The environmental challenges we face are global in nature and require cooperation across borders. Young environmental advocates often participate in international networks, where they share ideas, learn from each other's experiences, and collaborate on multinational projects. Conferences, summits, and online forums provide platforms for these interactions, helping to strengthen the global environmental movement.

Through these networks, young advocates gain insights into how environmental issues are tackled in different parts of the world.

This global perspective is invaluable in crafting effective and adaptable strategies for sustainability. It also fosters a sense of global citizenship and responsibility among young people, emphasizing that environmental advocacy is a shared endeavor.

Empowering Communities and Inspiring Change

One of the most significant impacts of young environmental advocates is their ability to inspire and empower others. By demonstrating leadership and commitment, they encourage peers and community members of all ages to take action for the environment. Through educational programs and community projects, they help others understand the importance of sustainability and the role each individual can play in achieving it.

Furthermore, by highlighting the interconnectedness of environmental issues with other societal concerns such as health, economic development, and social justice, young advocates broaden the appeal of the environmental movement. They make it clear that caring for the planet goes hand in hand with advancing human well-being.

Young environmental advocates are not only the voice of future generations; they are active participants in shaping a more sustainable world today. Their green dreams are grounded in a deep commitment to environmental stewardship and a belief in the power of collective action. As they continue to push for change, innovate, and lead, they remain a beacon of hope and a driving force behind the global movement towards a more sustainable and just planet.

ᗁᗁᗁ

"In classrooms across the world, young minds are
not just learning about history—they are preparing
to write it themselves. Their education is the
kindling for fires of change, sparking
transformations that will light up the world."

▷▷▷

TEN

VOICES OF THE FUTURE: YOUTH IN ADVOCACY AND SOCIAL MOVEMENTS

The voice of youth has always been a powerful force in shaping social change. Across history, young people have been at the forefront of many social movements, driving progress with their passion, energy, and unique perspectives. Today, this trend continues as youth around the world engage in advocacy and activism, addressing a wide range of issues from social justice and human rights to environmental sustainability and political reform. Their involvement is not just about making an immediate impact; it's about setting the stage for long-term changes that will define the future.

Youth advocacy and participation in social movements reflect a commitment to the principles of democracy and community. Young activists use their voices to champion the causes they believe in, often becoming catalysts for change within their societies. Their approach to activism is characterized by innovative strategies, inclusivity, and a deep understanding of the power of collective action.

Understanding the Motivations of Young Activists

Young people are often motivated to join advocacy and social movements by a sense of injustice or urgency regarding particular issues. This motivation is frequently rooted in personal experience or a deep empathy for others. As digital natives, today's youth are also highly influenced by the global connectivity provided by the internet, which exposes them to a wide range of issues and perspectives that transcend local and national boundaries.

This exposure can lead to a heightened sense of global awareness and a feeling of responsibility to contribute to global solutions. Additionally, the energy and idealism of youth can drive a more optimistic outlook on their ability to effect change, making them powerful advocates for issues that older generations may have accepted as intractable.

Strategies and Methods of Youth Activism

The methods by which young people engage in activism are diverse and continually evolving, especially with advancements in technology. Social media platforms have become significant tools for organizing, mobilizing, and raising awareness. These digital tools allow for rapid dissemination of information, coordination of actions across vast geographic areas, and real-time updates about ongoing movements.

Apart from digital activism, young people also engage in traditional forms of protest, such as marches, demonstrations, and public speaking. They often combine these methods with more creative forms of expression like art, music, and performance, which can make their messages more accessible and relatable to a broader audience.

Furthermore, youth activists are increasingly involved in policy-making processes, using formal channels to influence legislation and public policy. By engaging with local, national, and international bodies, they strive to translate their activism into concrete policy changes that institutionalize their goals.

Challenges Faced by Young Activists

Despite their enthusiasm and commitment, young activists often face significant challenges. These can include lack of access to resources, skepticism from older generations, and sometimes direct opposition or repression from those in power. Moreover, the intense involvement in advocacy work can lead to emotional and physical burnout, particularly if not managed with adequate support structures.

To overcome these challenges, many youth-led movements have developed networks that provide both logistical and emotional support. These networks can offer training, resources, and advice on how to engage effectively and safely in activism. Additionally, mentoring relationships with experienced activists can provide young people with valuable insights and guidance.

Impact and Contributions of Youth in Social Movements

The impact of youth on social movements can be profound. Not only do they contribute to immediate outcomes, such as policy changes or increased awareness, but they also play a crucial role in the cultural shifts that underpin long-term social transformation. By challenging established norms and proposing innovative solutions, young activists contribute to a dynamic reimagining of societal possibilities.

Moreover, youth activism often revitalizes broader social movements, infusing them with new energy and perspectives. This can help sustain movements over time, making them more adaptable and resilient to changing circumstances. The participation of young people also ensures that movements remain relevant to successive generations, fostering a culture of continuous engagement and vigilance that is necessary for the protection of rights and freedoms.

As voices of the future, young individuals in advocacy and social movements embody the evolving spirit of activism. They are not just participants but leaders who are shaping the contours of social justice and equity. Their proactive stance, innovative approaches, and resilience in the face of challenges make them formidable agents of change. As they continue to raise their voices and advocate for their causes, they inspire not only their peers but also older generations, highlighting the transformative power of engaged and informed youth in driving societal progress.

ᐅᐅᐅ

"The resilience of youth is a remarkable force,
sculpted by trials and kindled by challenges. Their
ability to bounce back and forge ahead carves out
new avenues for innovation and change."

ᗞᗞᗞ

ELEVEN

THE WORLD THROUGH THEIR EYES: GLOBAL PERSPECTIVES OF YOUNG THINKERS

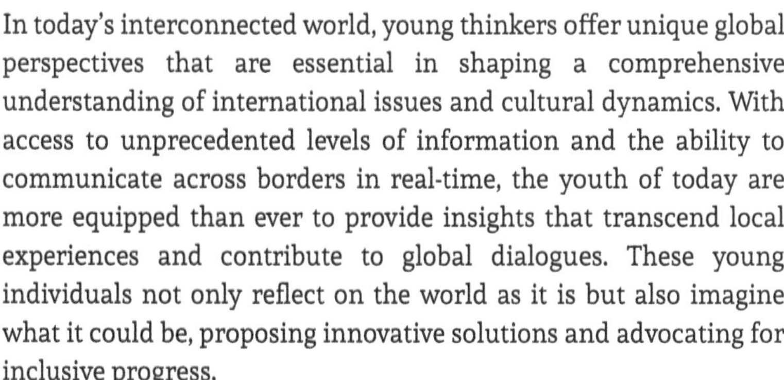

In today's interconnected world, young thinkers offer unique global perspectives that are essential in shaping a comprehensive understanding of international issues and cultural dynamics. With access to unprecedented levels of information and the ability to communicate across borders in real-time, the youth of today are more equipped than ever to provide insights that transcend local experiences and contribute to global dialogues. These young individuals not only reflect on the world as it is but also imagine what it could be, proposing innovative solutions and advocating for inclusive progress.

The diversity of thought among young thinkers from different parts of the world enriches global discussions, ensuring that multiple viewpoints are considered and that solutions are comprehensive and culturally sensitive. This diversity is crucial in tackling global challenges such as climate change, economic inequality, and social justice, which require cooperation across national and cultural boundaries.

Exposure and Empathy: Building a Global Mindset

The global perspective of young thinkers is largely shaped by their exposure to varied cultures, languages, and ideas. This exposure often comes through education, travel, media, and increasingly, through digital connectivity. Online platforms and social networks allow young people to interact with peers from around the world, sharing experiences and viewpoints that broaden their understanding and foster empathy.

Empathy plays a critical role in shaping the global perspectives of young thinkers. By understanding the struggles and aspirations of people from different backgrounds, young individuals develop a more nuanced view of the world. This empathetic approach encourages a sense of global citizenship, where the challenges of one part of the world are seen as relevant and important to all.

Challenges and Opportunities in a Globalized World

Young thinkers are keenly aware of the challenges posed by globalization, including economic disparity, cultural homogenization, and environmental sustainability. They often question traditional approaches and push for new ways of thinking about and addressing these issues. For instance, in discussions about economic development, young thinkers might advocate for models that prioritize sustainability and equity over short-term gains.

The opportunities presented by globalization are also eagerly embraced by young individuals. They see potential for collaborative projects that leverage diverse skills and perspectives, and they advocate for policies that promote international cooperation and understanding. In many cases, young thinkers are at the forefront of initiatives that use technology to solve global problems, such as apps that connect donors to causes worldwide or platforms that offer educational resources to underserved populations.

Bridging the Gap: From Insight to Action

The transition from insight to action is a vital step for young thinkers who are eager to make a tangible impact. Many engage in advocacy, volunteering, or entrepreneurship as means to apply their global perspectives in constructive ways. They work in NGOs, start social enterprises, or collaborate with international organizations to implement projects that reflect their understanding of global issues.

The ability to think globally also informs their approach to leadership and decision-making. Young leaders who see the world through a global lens are more likely to consider the long-term impacts of their decisions and prioritize inclusivity and sustainability. They often advocate for policies and practices that are not only beneficial locally but also contribute positively to global well-being.

The Role of Education and Policy in Shaping Global Thinkers

Educational institutions and policies play crucial roles in nurturing the global perspectives of young thinkers. Curriculums that include international history, languages, and studies on global issues are fundamental in broadening young minds. Exchange programs and international collaborations further enhance this global outlook by providing firsthand experiences of diverse cultures and governance structures.

Policymakers are also encouraged to support initiatives that facilitate global education and exchange. By investing in such programs, governments can ensure that the next generation is well-equipped to handle the challenges of an increasingly globalized world. Moreover, involving young people in policy dialogues and decision-making processes at the international level can help harness their insights and energy in shaping global agendas.

Cultivating a Network of Global Young Thinkers

The cultivation of a global network of young thinkers is essential for the continued exchange of ideas and collaborative problem-solving. Such networks provide platforms for dialogue, partnership, and mutual learning, strengthening the global community's ability to address complex challenges. These networks not only foster professional relationships but also build friendships that bridge cultural divides, laying the foundation for a more peaceful and cooperative world.

The global perspectives of young thinkers are invaluable in navigating the complexities of today's world. Their unique insights and innovative approaches contribute to a richer, more inclusive dialogue on international issues. By embracing and fostering these perspectives, societies can better prepare for a future that is shaped by understanding, cooperation, and shared responsibility. As these young individuals move into positions of influence, their global outlook will continue to drive positive change and inspire a more connected and empathetic world community.

ᏇᏇᏇ

"Mentorship bridges the gap between generations,
turning wisdom into action and dreams into
realities. It is in these connections that young
minds find the strength to leap towards their
aspirations."

ᗷᗷᗷ

TWELVE

EDUCATION REIMAGINED: THE ROLE OF YOUTH IN SHAPING LEARNING

In an era where traditional educational systems often struggle to keep pace with rapid technological advancements and cultural shifts, the role of youth in shaping education is more critical than ever. Young people, as both recipients and increasingly as contributors to the educational dialogue, are instrumental in driving the evolution of learning environments and pedagogies. Their unique insights into the demands of the modern world, coupled with their natural affinity for technology, position them uniquely to redefine what learning looks like in the 21st century.

Today's youth are not just passive participants in their education; they are active agents seeking to tailor learning experiences to better meet their needs and the needs of their communities. From advocating for inclusive curriculums to integrating technology into the classroom, young people are at the forefront of educational innovation.

Harnessing Technology to Transform Learning

One of the most significant areas where youth are reshaping education is through the integration of technology. Digital natives, young people often lead the way in utilizing new technologies to enhance learning. This includes everything from using educational apps and platforms to facilitate learning to leveraging social media for educational purposes and creating digital content that supplements traditional learning materials.

For instance, the use of virtual reality (VR) and augmented reality (AR) in classrooms has been championed by tech-savvy students, offering immersive experiences that bring abstract concepts to life. Similarly, the use of artificial intelligence (AI) in personalized learning is another area where young innovators are making significant impacts, designing systems that adapt to the learning pace and style of individual students.

Advocating for Inclusive and Diverse Curriculums

Young people are also vocal advocates for inclusivity and diversity in educational content. They push for curriculums that reflect a wider range of perspectives and histories, including more comprehensive representations of gender, race, culture, and sexuality. This advocacy not only involves lobbying for changes in textbooks and teaching materials but also extends to the inclusivity of the learning environment itself, ensuring that schools are safe spaces for all students.

Furthermore, youth activism in education often focuses on making learning accessible to all, advocating for policies and practices that address educational disparities. This includes campaigning for adequate resources in underfunded schools, supporting special education, and enhancing language support for non-native speakers.

Rethinking Pedagogy: Student-Centered Learning

Another significant contribution of youth to the reimagining of education lies in their push for student-centered learning approaches. Young learners advocate for a shift away from rote memorization and standardized testing towards methods that emphasize critical thinking, problem-solving, and creativity. These approaches allow students to take charge of their learning, giving them more autonomy over what and how they learn, which can lead to increased motivation and engagement.

Project-based learning, experiential learning, and inquiry-based learning are examples of educational methodologies that have gained traction under the influence of student input and participation. These methods not only make learning more relevant and exciting but also help students develop essential life skills such as collaboration, communication, and resilience.

Building Learning Communities Beyond Classrooms

Youth are also expanding the concept of learning communities beyond traditional classroom settings. They utilize online platforms to create global classrooms where students from around the world can collaborate on projects, share insights, and learn from one another. This global exchange enriches students' educational experiences by exposing them to different cultures and viewpoints, fostering global citizenship.

Moreover, young people are creating and participating in mentorship programs that connect students with professionals and experts who can offer guidance, career advice, and real-world experience related to their fields of interest. These mentorship opportunities not only enhance educational outcomes but also help students navigate future career paths.

Leading Educational Change Through Entrepreneurship

Finally, young educational entrepreneurs are designing products and services that address gaps in the current educational system. From startups that develop educational technologies to non-profits that work to improve educational access and quality for disadvantaged groups, young leaders are at the helm of many initiatives that are directly shaping the landscape of education.

These entrepreneurial ventures not only provide innovative solutions to enduring challenges but also inspire a culture of creativity and self-efficacy among students, showing them that they have the power to effect change not only in their own educational journeys but also in the broader educational system.

The role of youth in shaping education is characterized by a forward-thinking, inclusive approach that harnesses technology, advocates for diversity, and promotes student-centered learning. As educators and policymakers begin to recognize the valuable insights and contributions of young people, the collaborative efforts between different generations are likely to lead to more dynamic, responsive, and effective educational systems. These systems will not only better serve the diverse needs of students but will also equip them with the skills and knowledge required to thrive in an increasingly complex world.

ᐅᐅᐅ

"Youth activism is the bold stroke that paints the future in vibrant hues of justice and equality. Each campaign, each protest, each call to action repaints the canvas of society."

THIRTEEN

The Ethics of Ambition: Balancing Drive and Compassion

Ambition is often celebrated as a driving force behind personal success and societal progress. It motivates individuals to strive for excellence and achieve goals that may seem beyond reach. However, when ambition is pursued without ethical considerations, it can lead to behaviors and decisions that harm others and the environment. Thus, understanding how to balance ambition with compassion is essential for fostering a society that values both achievement and ethical integrity.

This balance is particularly relevant in today's fast-paced, competitive world, where the pressure to succeed can sometimes overshadow the importance of fairness, empathy, and responsibility. Young individuals, who are at the formative stages of their career and personal development, must navigate these waters with a keen sense of ethics to ensure that their drive to succeed does not compromise their values.

Defining Ethical Ambition

Ethical ambition can be defined as the pursuit of success while adhering to core values such as honesty, respect, and fairness. It involves setting goals that not only lead to personal advancement but also contribute positively to the well-being of others and the broader community. This concept challenges the traditional notion that ambition and ethics are at odds, proposing instead that they can coexist and even complement each other.

Incorporating ethics into ambition means making decisions that reflect one's values, even when faced with opportunities to achieve faster success by questionable means. It requires a conscious effort to consider the consequences of one's actions on others and the environment. Ethical leaders, for instance, strive to achieve business success without exploiting their employees, customers, or the planet. They seek profits, but not at the cost of their integrity or societal well-being.

Balancing Personal Drive with Social Responsibility

The balance between personal ambition and social responsibility is a delicate one. It requires individuals to be self-aware and reflective about the motivations behind their ambitions and the impact of their actions. Education plays a crucial role in cultivating this balance, by instilling ethical reasoning and empathy from an early age.

Schools and universities can incorporate discussions about ethics into various subjects, not limited to philosophy or social studies. For example, business courses can include case studies on ethical dilemmas in the corporate world, while science classes can discuss the social implications of technological advancements.

Compassion as a Guiding Principle

Compassion is a powerful counterbalance to ambition. It encourages individuals to consider the broader impact of their pursuit of success and to care about the well-being of others. Compassionate leaders are motivated to succeed not just for personal gain but to improve the lives of others. Their ambitions drive them to innovate and excel, but their compassion ensures that their methods and outcomes are beneficial to all.

Fostering a culture of compassion within organizations and institutions is essential for encouraging ethical ambition. This can be achieved through leadership that models compassionate behavior, policies that promote fairness and inclusivity, and community engagement initiatives that keep the organization connected to the needs of the people it serves.

The Role of Mentorship in Ethical Ambition

Mentorship is another key element in fostering ethical ambition. Mentors can guide young individuals to set goals that are ambitious yet ethical and to navigate the challenges that come with striving for success in a competitive world. They can provide not only career guidance but also ethical guidance, sharing their experiences of facing and overcoming ethical dilemmas.

Mentors also play a critical role in shaping the culture of organizations and fields by transmitting values and norms to the next generation. By choosing mentors who exemplify ethical ambition, young people can learn how to integrate these principles into their own career paths.

Challenges in Practicing Ethical Ambition

Practicing ethical ambition is not without challenges. There can be significant pressure to cut corners, overlook unethical behavior, or prioritize personal gain over communal well-being, especially in highly competitive environments. Additionally, the ambiguity in ethical dilemmas can make it difficult to determine the right course of action.

To navigate these challenges, it is crucial for individuals to develop a strong ethical framework and seek diverse perspectives when faced with difficult choices. Regular reflection and dialogue about ethics with peers, mentors, and through professional development opportunities can reinforce an individual's ability to maintain ethical standards.

The ethics of ambition involves a complex balancing act between personal drive and compassion. By fostering ethical ambition, society can benefit from the achievements of individuals who not only reach their personal goals but also contribute positively to the world. As young individuals progress in their careers and personal lives, embedding ethical considerations into their ambitions will be essential for building a just, successful, and sustainable society.

ϷϷϷ

"In the spirit of entrepreneurial ventures, young minds see not just opportunities but solutions for a better world. Their businesses are more than profit-driven—they are purpose-driven."

ᗽᗽᗽ

FOURTEEN

MENTORSHIP AND ITS MAGIC: LEARNING FROM THE EXPERIENCED

Mentorship is a powerful tool that bridges generations, transferring knowledge, skills, and values in a personal and impactful way. It goes beyond mere teaching or training; it is a relationship built on trust, guidance, and mutual respect, where experienced individuals help guide others through the complexities of professional and personal development. The magic of mentorship lies in its ability to transform lives, shaping mentees' careers and character by providing them with tailored advice, support, and the wisdom of experience.

This dynamic process benefits not just the mentees but also mentors, who gain fresh perspectives and the satisfaction of contributing to someone else's growth. As such, mentorship enriches both participants, creating lasting bonds and a legacy of knowledge sharing that can influence multiple generations.

The Role of Mentorship in Professional Growth

In professional contexts, mentors help navigate the often-turbulent waters of career development. For young professionals, navigating industry landscapes filled with both opportunities and pitfalls can be daunting. Mentors act as compasses, offering guidance drawn from their own experiences. They can advise on everything from strategic career moves to workplace dynamics, helping mentees avoid common mistakes and maximize their opportunities.

Moreover, mentors provide a network of professional contacts that can open doors for young professionals. This aspect of mentorship is invaluable as it can significantly accelerate career progression. By introducing mentees to industry contacts, mentors help them build their own networks, essential for career advancement.

Personal Development Through Mentorship

Beyond professional growth, mentorship profoundly impacts personal development. Mentors often become role models, influencing not just the professional choices of their mentees but also their values and ethical standards. Through their behavior and the stories they share, mentors exemplify how to balance ambition with integrity, how to face challenges with resilience, and how to interact with others respectfully and compassionately.

This personal guidance is crucial during times of uncertainty or transition. Mentors provide support and reassurance, helping mentees to see beyond temporary setbacks and focus on long-term goals. They encourage personal reflection, which is vital for self-improvement and emotional growth.

Developing Soft Skills Through Mentorship

Mentorship also plays a key role in developing soft skills, which are increasingly recognized as critical for success in any field. These include communication, leadership, problem-solving, and teamwork skills. Mentors help hone these skills through one-on-one interactions, feedback, and by providing opportunities for mentees to practice these skills in real-world situations.

For instance, a mentor might coach a mentee on how to effectively communicate in the workplace, providing tips on everything from how to write professional emails to how to negotiate with colleagues. They might also provide leadership opportunities, such as leading a team project or presenting at a meeting, with constructive feedback that helps the mentee improve.

The Evolving Nature of Mentorship

While traditional mentorship involves face-to-face interactions, technological advancements have transformed how this guidance can be delivered. Virtual mentorship has become increasingly common, facilitated by digital tools that allow for remote communication. This has expanded the possibilities for mentorship, enabling connections that are not limited by geographical boundaries.

Furthermore, the concept of reverse mentorship, where younger employees mentor older executives, particularly in areas like technology and current trends, is gaining traction. This form of mentorship recognizes that learning is a two-way street and that fresh perspectives can invigorate even the most seasoned professionals.

Challenges and Rewards of Being a Mentor

Being a mentor comes with its own set of challenges and rewards. Mentors must be patient and empathetic, willing to invest time and energy into another person's growth without immediate personal benefit. They must also be open to learning themselves, as teaching others often provides new insights into their own experiences and assumptions.

The rewards of mentorship, however, are profound. Mentors often express a deep sense of fulfillment from helping others succeed. Watching a mentee grow, overcome challenges, and achieve their goals can be incredibly gratifying. Moreover, the relationship developed through mentorship can evolve into a lifelong friendship, enriching both the mentor's and the mentee's lives.

Mentorship is a transformative practice that benefits both the mentor and the mentee. It is a symbiotic relationship that fosters professional and personal development, enriches careers, and cultivates new generations of skilled and ethical leaders. By continuing to embrace and promote the culture of mentorship, industries and communities can ensure the passing of invaluable knowledge and the continuation of legacy through the magic of learning from the experienced.

ᗏᗏᗏ

"Every young creator who challenges the norm is rewriting the rules for the next generation. Their courage to defy and redefine boundaries is what propels society forward."

♥♥♥

FIFTEEN

BUILDING RESILIENCE: COPING WITH FAILURE AND SETBACKS

Resilience is the capacity to recover quickly from difficulties; it's a crucial quality that enables individuals to navigate the inevitable challenges and setbacks they encounter in life. This capacity is not innate; rather, it is cultivated through experiences and deliberate practice. For many, the journey to building resilience begins with learning how to cope effectively with failure. Embracing failures as opportunities for growth rather than signs of defeat is essential for anyone who aims to thrive in both their personal and professional lives.

Understanding the Nature of Failure

Failure is an integral part of the human experience. In many ways, how one deals with failure can define their path more significantly than how they handle success. It is important to recognize that failure is not a reflection of one's worth but rather a natural outcome of taking risks and trying new things. Normalizing failure as a part of the learning process is the first step towards building resilience.

When individuals understand that failure is not catastrophic but an opportunity to gain insights, they are more likely to approach challenges with a mindset that embraces rather than fears potential setbacks. This shift in perspective is crucial for developing the tenacity needed to persevere through difficult times.

Strategies for Coping with Failure

Developing effective strategies for coping with failure is crucial for building resilience. One such strategy is maintaining a growth mindset—a belief that abilities and intelligence can be developed through dedication and hard work. Individuals with a growth mindset perceive challenges as opportunities to improve, making them more likely to learn from their mistakes.

Another strategy involves setting realistic expectations and achievable goals. When goals are set too high or are unrealistic, failure is more likely, and the impact can be discouraging. By setting achievable milestones, individuals can enjoy the satisfaction of accomplishment, which builds confidence and fortitude to tackle more significant challenges.

Emotional Resilience: Managing Reactions to Setbacks

Emotional resilience refers to the ability to emotionally cope with crises and return to pre-crisis status quickly. Developing emotional resilience involves several key practices:

Self-awareness: Understanding one's emotional responses to setbacks is crucial. Recognizing emotions like frustration, disappointment, or sadness when they arise and acknowledging them without judgment allows individuals to manage these feelings more effectively.

Self-care: Regular physical activity, adequate sleep, healthy eating, and mindfulness practices like meditation can strengthen one's overall emotional health, making it easier to deal with stress and setbacks.

Social support: Having a robust support network can provide emotional comfort and practical assistance during tough times. Sharing experiences with others who understand and can offer perspective and encouragement makes burdens easier to bear.

Learning from Failure

To truly build resilience, one must learn from failure. This involves analyzing what went wrong, identifying the factors that led to the failure, and determining what can be done differently in the future. This reflective process turns setbacks into valuable learning experiences.

It is also helpful to maintain a journal or log of failures and their subsequent analyses. This record not only tracks progress over time but also provides tangible evidence that past failures have been overcome, boosting confidence in handling future challenges.

Encouraging Resilience in Others

Building resilience is not just an individual endeavor. Parents, teachers, mentors, and leaders have roles to play in encouraging resilience in others. This can be achieved by:

Modeling resilient behavior: Demonstrating how to cope with setbacks in one's own life can provide a real-life example for others to follow.

Providing opportunities for small risks: Encouraging others to take on challenges that carry a risk of failure helps them practice resilience in a controlled, supportive environment.

Offering constructive feedback: Instead of criticism, provide feedback that focuses on efforts and improvement rather than on the failure itself.

Resilience is a fundamental quality that enables individuals to thrive despite the adversities they face. By understanding the nature of failure, developing effective coping strategies, learning from setbacks, and fostering a supportive environment, individuals can build the resilience needed to face future challenges with confidence. This process of building resilience not only prepares one for personal and professional challenges but also enriches their overall life experience, making them more robust, compassionate, and understanding individuals.

PPP

"Technology in the hands of the youth is a powerful equalizer, breaking down barriers and building bridges. It is their tool of choice for crafting a world where access and opportunities abound."

❦❦❦

SIXTEEN

BEYOND BOUNDARIES: THE IMPACT OF YOUNG EXPLORERS

In a world increasingly connected yet divided by invisible lines of culture, politics, and geography, young explorers are pushing the limits, both literally and metaphorically. These intrepid individuals—travelers, researchers, and adventurers—venture beyond familiar territories to bring back not just tales of the unknown but also insights that can bridge gaps and foster a greater understanding among diverse populations. Their journeys serve as catalysts for change, challenging preconceived notions and expanding the global dialogue.

Young explorers impact the world in numerous ways, from contributing to scientific discoveries and environmental conservation to enhancing cultural exchanges and global awareness. Their work and experiences are vital in promoting a connected world where knowledge flows freely and barriers are progressively dismantled.

Scientific Exploration and Environmental Awareness

Many young explorers are drawn to the natural sciences, where they contribute to vital research on climate change, biodiversity, and sustainability. By traveling to remote corners of the Earth, these young scientists collect data crucial for understanding environmental changes and their impacts on local and global scales. Their work often leads to important discoveries about ecosystems and wildlife, providing essential insights for conservation efforts.

For instance, young biologists trekking through untouched rainforests may discover new species, adding to our biodiversity knowledge bank and informing conservation strategies. Similarly, marine biologists diving into unexplored waters help illuminate the mysterious lifeforms of the ocean, which is essential for marine conservation.

Cultural Exchange and Global Understanding

Beyond the sciences, young explorers also make significant contributions to cultural understanding. Through their travels and interactions, they engage with different communities, learning and sharing stories, customs, and traditions. This exchange of cultural knowledge is crucial in an increasingly globalized world as it fosters mutual respect and understanding among diverse populations.

These young individuals often document their experiences through blogs, videos, and social media, sharing their journey with a global audience. This not only educates others but also promotes tolerance and appreciation for cultural diversity. Moreover, it inspires more young people to explore, creating a cycle of learning and discovery that enriches global youth culture.

Adventurers and the Human Spirit

The tales of young adventurers also serve to remind us of the vast capabilities of the human spirit. These individuals often face significant physical and mental challenges, from scaling rugged mountains to navigating treacherous waters. Their achievements not only push the boundaries of human endurance but also inspire others to explore their own limits and capabilities.

The stories of these adventurers can be particularly motivating for young people. They demonstrate that with determination and resilience, it is possible to overcome daunting challenges and achieve extraordinary things. This can be a powerful lesson in personal development and self-belief.

Technological Innovation in Exploration

Technology plays a significant role in modern exploration, and young explorers are often at the forefront of utilizing and sometimes developing these technologies. From sophisticated navigation systems and drones to advanced communication tools and wearable tech, these tools enable deeper and safer exploration than ever before.

Young tech-savvy explorers not only use these tools but also innovate them. For example, a young explorer might develop a new mapping app that helps hikers track their routes more accurately or a new type of eco-friendly gear that makes expeditions less harmful to the environment. These technological advancements contribute to the field of exploration and open up more possibilities for future explorers.

Challenges and Ethical Considerations

The path of an explorer is not without its challenges. These range from physical dangers and financial constraints to ethical dilemmas about interacting with indigenous cultures and impacting delicate ecosystems. Young explorers must navigate these challenges thoughtfully, ensuring that their quests for knowledge and adventure do not harm the people or places they aim to learn about.

Responsible exploration involves preparing adequately, respecting local customs and regulations, and minimizing environmental impact. It also entails sharing findings in ways that respect the privacy and dignity of local communities, especially when disseminating information and images globally.

Young explorers make profound contributions to science, culture, and our understanding of the human capacity. Their endeavors not only broaden their own horizons but also enrich the global community with new knowledge and mutual respect. By pushing beyond boundaries, these young individuals play a critical role in bridging worlds, fostering global dialogue, and inspiring future generations to explore, understand, and cherish our complex and beautiful planet. Their journeys remind us that there are always new things to learn, places to see, and bridges to build, as long as we are willing to venture beyond the familiar.

"The creativity of young minds fuels the engines of cultural evolution. Through their art, music, and stories, they invite us to see the world through a kaleidoscope of perspectives."

❦❦❦

SEVENTEEN

CULTURAL CONNECTORS: YOUTH PROMOTING DIVERSITY AND INCLUSION

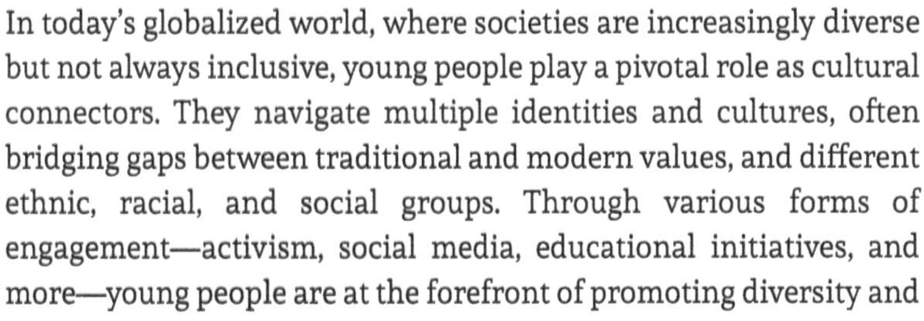

In today's globalized world, where societies are increasingly diverse but not always inclusive, young people play a pivotal role as cultural connectors. They navigate multiple identities and cultures, often bridging gaps between traditional and modern values, and different ethnic, racial, and social groups. Through various forms of engagement—activism, social media, educational initiatives, and more—young people are at the forefront of promoting diversity and fostering a culture of inclusion.

The work of these young cultural connectors is crucial for creating communities that value diversity as a strength rather than a source of division. Their efforts help combat prejudice and discrimination, enabling societies to harness the full potential of their diverse populations.

Understanding Diversity and Inclusion

Before delving into the roles young people play in promoting diversity and inclusion, it's important to understand these concepts. Diversity refers to the range of human differences, including but not limited to race, ethnicity, gender, age, social class, physical ability or attributes, religious or ethical values system, national origin, and political beliefs. Inclusion, on the other hand, involves bringing together and harnessing these diverse forces and resources in a way that is beneficial. It's about actively inviting the contribution and participation of all people. Effective inclusion results in a feeling of belonging and mutual respect among community members, something young cultural connectors strive to achieve.

Youth as Drivers of Cultural Exchange

Young people often find themselves at the intersection of various cultural currents, making them natural cultural connectors. Many grow up with multiple cultural influences — navigating and merging different cultural identities allows them to naturally foster understanding and tolerance among diverse groups.

In schools and universities, young cultural connectors initiate and lead a variety of cultural exchange programs and multicultural events that celebrate different cultures. Through food festivals, language days, art exhibitions, and discussion forums, they provide platforms for students to share their heritage and learn about others. These activities not only educate but also dismantle stereotypes, building bridges of understanding.

Leveraging Technology for Inclusion

In the digital age, young cultural connectors utilize technology to promote diversity and inclusion on a scale never before possible. Social media platforms allow them to reach a global audience, sharing stories that highlight the beauty of diversity and the importance of inclusion. They create content that challenges racial stereotypes, promotes gender equality, and advocates for the rights of marginalized communities.

Moreover, young innovators are developing apps and platforms that enhance accessibility for people with disabilities, connect refugees with essential services, and facilitate the integration of immigrant populations into new communities. These technological solutions not only address immediate needs but also promote long-term inclusion.

Advocacy and Policy Influence

Young cultural connectors are not only active at the community and digital levels but also in the policymaking arena. They advocate for policies that promote diversity and inclusion in education, healthcare, employment, and housing. By participating in debates, speaking at public hearings, and working with inclusive organizations, they influence local, national, and international policies.

These young activists understand that for diversity and inclusion efforts to be sustainable, they must be institutionalized. Thus, they work to ensure that diversity and inclusion are not just buzzwords but integral aspects of policy frameworks.

Challenges and Resilience in Advocacy

The path of advocating for diversity and inclusion is fraught with challenges. Cultural connectors often face resistance from conservative factions within societies. They encounter pushback against changes that promote equality and inclusiveness, especially when such changes challenge long-standing norms and power structures.

However, the resilience displayed by young cultural connectors is noteworthy. They persevere in their advocacy efforts despite setbacks, using every platform available to advance their cause. Their resilience is fueled by a deep belief in the value of a diverse and inclusive society, as well as the tangible benefits it brings—increased creativity, stronger communities, and greater equality.

Young cultural connectors play an indispensable role in transforming societies. Through their efforts in cultural exchange, technological innovation, and policy advocacy, they promote a more inclusive understanding of diversity. They challenge societal norms, push for systemic change, and pave the way for a more inclusive world. By valuing every individual's unique contributions and creating spaces where everyone can thrive, young cultural connectors not only enrich their communities but also inspire future generations to continue the work of making society more inclusive for all.

קקק

"Young scholars are not merely students of the world; they are its next great teachers. Their research and discoveries are the keys unlocking solutions to the world's most pressing challenges."

ppp

EIGHTEEN

TECH FOR GOOD: ETHICAL INNOVATIONS BY YOUNG MINDS

In the realm of technology, the narrative often revolves around disruption and innovation for profit and efficiency. However, an emerging and compelling storyline is the rise of "Tech for Good"—a movement where technology is intentionally designed and used to address social, environmental, and ethical challenges. Young innovators are increasingly at the forefront of this movement, leveraging their technological prowess and creativity to develop solutions that not only push the boundaries of what technology can achieve but also prioritize the welfare of society and the environment.

This focus on ethical innovation reflects a broader shift in how technology is perceived and utilized by the younger generation. They see technology not just as a tool for individual advancement but as a means to promote collective well-being, demonstrating a profound commitment to using their skills for societal benefit.

The Foundation of Ethical Innovation

The concept of ethical innovation in technology encompasses a wide range of practices—from the development of products that enhance accessibility and inclusivity to algorithms designed to eliminate bias rather than perpetuate it. At its core, ethical innovation involves the consideration of the broader impacts of technology on people and the planet. It requires thinking beyond the traditional metrics of success, like speed and profit, to include values such as fairness, privacy, and sustainability.

Young tech innovators are embedding these values into their projects from the outset. They are building apps that improve accessibility for people with disabilities, platforms that facilitate transparent and fair trade in developing economies, and systems that leverage data to tackle issues like climate change and health disparities.

Promoting Inclusivity and Accessibility

One significant area of focus for young innovators is the use of technology to enhance inclusivity and accessibility. This includes the development of assistive devices that use AI to help individuals with visual or auditory impairments navigate their environments more independently. For instance, apps that convert speech to text in real time can transform classroom experiences for students who are deaf or hard of hearing, allowing them to participate more fully in their education.

Furthermore, young developers are creating virtual reality (VR) experiences that enable people from different cultural backgrounds to experience each other's worlds, promoting empathy and understanding across divides. These VR experiences can transport users to far-flung communities, allowing them to witness the impacts of climate change or see the world through the eyes of someone from a different socioeconomic status or culture.

Tackling Environmental Challenges

Environmental sustainability is another critical area where young tech innovators are making substantial impacts. They are using technology to create solutions that help mitigate the effects of climate change, promote sustainable agriculture, and reduce waste. For example, IoT (Internet of Things) technologies enable more efficient resource management, from smart grids that optimize energy use to agricultural sensors that help farmers use water and fertilizers more efficiently.

Moreover, young innovators are also focusing on the development of clean technologies, such as renewable energy systems and biodegradable materials, that aim to reduce pollution and conserve the environment. These technologies are not only beneficial for the planet but also provide sustainable business models that challenge traditional industries to innovate towards greener alternatives.

Ethical Data Use and AI

The ethical use of data and artificial intelligence is a complex and urgent issue that young tech innovators are actively addressing. They are at the helm of designing algorithms that prioritize fairness and transparency. This includes efforts to eliminate biases in AI applications, from facial recognition software to decision-making systems used in hiring, lending, and law enforcement.

Young developers are also advocating for and creating more robust privacy protections to ensure that the collection and use of data do not infringe on individual rights. They are building decentralized systems that give users more control over their data and using blockchain technology to enhance security and transparency in transactions.

Challenges and the Path Forward

Despite their passion and ingenuity, young innovators face significant challenges, including limited access to capital, resistance from established industries, and regulatory hurdles. Additionally, there is the constant challenge of ensuring that technology developed for good does not inadvertently cause harm, a risk that requires ongoing assessment and adaptation.

To overcome these challenges, young innovators often rely on a combination of community building, advocacy, and collaboration with like-minded organizations and mentors who can provide guidance and support. They also focus on educating others about the importance of ethical innovation, building a broader base of support for their initiatives.

The movement of "Tech for Good" spearheaded by young minds is a testament to the potential of technology to make a positive impact on the world. Through their commitment to ethical innovation, these young individuals are not only developing new technologies but are also redefining the goals and values of the tech industry. Their work is crucial in ensuring that the tech advancements of the future are aligned with the needs and welfare of society, paving the way for a more equitable and sustainable world. Through their efforts, technology becomes not just a tool for economic growth but a true force for good.

ᐅᐅᐅ

"In the narratives of young influencers, media becomes a mirror reflecting the society we aspire to create. They curate content with the power to shift perceptions and dismantle stereotypes."

ᐁᐁᐁ

NINETEEN

THE SOUNDTRACK OF CHANGE: YOUNG VOICES IN MUSIC AND MEDIA

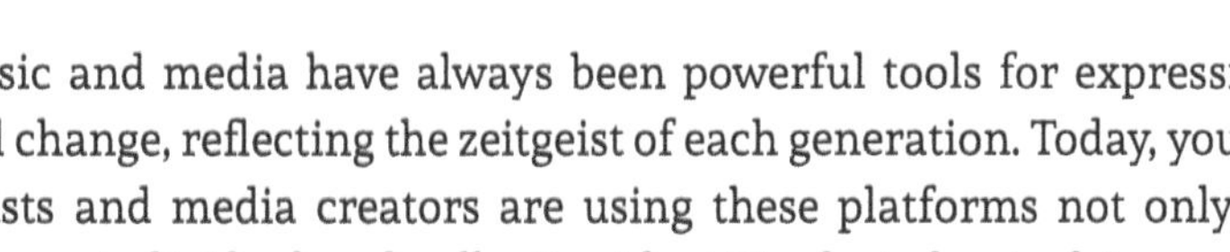

Music and media have always been powerful tools for expression and change, reflecting the zeitgeist of each generation. Today, young artists and media creators are using these platforms not only to express individual and collective identities but also to drive social and political change. Through innovative approaches to music and media, they are shaping public discourse, challenging societal norms, and inspiring a global audience to think and act differently.

Harnessing Music for Social Impact

Music has a unique ability to transcend language barriers and connect people emotionally. Young musicians today are acutely aware of this power and leverage it to address topics ranging from mental health and social justice to environmental concerns. By infusing their music with messages about important issues, these artists raise awareness and encourage action among their listeners.

For instance, songs addressing climate change, such as those inspired by movements like Fridays for Future, can mobilize listeners by conveying urgency and the emotional weight of the crisis. Similarly, music that tackles themes of equality and human rights can play a crucial role in influencing public sentiment and inspiring solidarity. These young musicians often collaborate with activists and NGOs, using concerts and albums as platforms to raise funds and awareness for various causes.

Transforming Media Narratives

In the realm of media, young creators are redefining traditional formats and channels to better reflect the diversity and dynamics of contemporary society. This generation of media influencers utilizes platforms like YouTube, TikTok, and podcasts to reach a global audience, share their narratives, and challenge mainstream media's status quo.

These young media creators are keenly aware of the power of representation and strive to provide a space for voices that are often marginalized. Whether it's through creating content that highlights the stories of minority communities, or through advocating for inclusivity in media production and storytelling, these young creators are making the media landscape more diverse and equitable.

Advocacy Through Artistic Collaboration

Collaboration is a significant aspect of how young voices in music and media amplify their impact. By joining forces, artists and creators can combine their talents and platforms to reach wider audiences and tackle issues from multiple angles. Collaborative projects, such as benefit concerts, collaborative singles, or social media campaigns, harness the collective influence of several artists, which can lead to greater engagement and a stronger call to action.

These collaborations often extend beyond artists to include partnerships with activists, nonprofits, and even brands that want to associate with socially responsible messages. Such partnerships can provide the necessary resources for large-scale projects that have the potential to make a significant impact.

Innovating with Technology

Technology plays a crucial role in how young creators produce and disseminate their work. Advances in digital audio workstations, streaming services, and social media platforms enable artists to create high-quality content from virtually anywhere, bypass barriers to traditional media distribution, and engage with audiences directly.

In music, technology allows for the creation of new sounds and the resurrection of old styles in modern formats, making music a continually evolving art form. In media, technology enables the creation of immersive experiences—such as virtual reality (VR) documentaries—that can transport viewers to different times and places, deepening their understanding of complex issues.

Challenges and Resilience

Despite their passion and innovation, young artists and media creators face challenges, including economic constraints, censorship, and the pressure to conform to commercial expectations. Moreover, the digital landscape, while offering numerous opportunities, also presents challenges like information overload and the rapid spread of misinformation.

Nevertheless, the resilience shown by these young creators is remarkable. They adapt to new technologies, navigate changing market dynamics, and continue to find inventive ways to express themselves and reach their audiences. Their commitment to their art and their messages drives them to keep pushing boundaries and exploring new ways to make an impact.

Young voices in music and media are powerful agents of change. Through their creative expressions, they are not only defining the cultural landscape of their generation but are also actively participating in the broader social and political dialogues. By harnessing the power of music and media, these young creators continue to inspire, challenge, and lead in the pursuit of a more just and compassionate world. Their work is a testament to the enduring power of the arts as a catalyst for change, and their voices will likely resonate for generations to come, shaping the soundtrack of change and guiding society towards greater understanding and action.

"The power of young voices in advocacy is not just in speaking out but in being heard. Their words are the seeds from which grows a garden of societal change."

ꕤꕤꕤ

TWENTY

Looking Ahead: Preparing for a World Transformed by Youth

As the world undergoes rapid transformations across technological, environmental, and socio-political landscapes, the role of youth in shaping the future becomes increasingly central. Young individuals, empowered by unprecedented access to information and new technologies, are not just adapting to changes; they are actively driving them. Preparing for a world transformed by youth involves recognizing and fostering the unique contributions of younger generations, adapting traditional systems to new realities, and embracing a future where innovation and inclusivity are paramount.

Understanding the Influence of Youth Today

Youth today are distinguished by their digital nativity, global interconnectedness, and progressive attitudes toward diversity and inclusion. They grow up in a world where information is at their fingertips and global communication is instantaneous. These conditions have not only shaped their worldviews but have also equipped them with tools to influence change directly and effectively.

Recognizing the influence of youth involves understanding their values and concerns, which often include climate change, social justice, mental health, and economic stability. These priorities reflect broader global challenges and highlight the areas where young people are most likely to invest their energies and innovation.

Education Systems Adapting to New Realities

One of the critical areas requiring adaptation to harness the potential of youth is education. Traditional educational models, often criticized for being too rigid or out-of-touch, are being reevaluated to better suit the needs and skills of the digital age. This involves not only integrating technology into classrooms but also revamping curricula to include critical thinking, digital literacy, and interdisciplinary studies that reflect real-world issues.

Furthermore, education systems are increasingly focusing on soft skills such as teamwork, communication, and adaptability—skills that are crucial in a rapidly changing world. These systems are also beginning to incorporate experiential learning opportunities that allow students to engage directly with the industries and issues they are passionate about, providing real-world experience and fostering a deeper understanding of global challenges.

The Role of Policy in Empowering Youth

Policy makers play a crucial role in preparing for a world transformed by youth. This involves creating policies that not only address the immediate needs of young people but also empower them to participate in decision-making processes. By involving youth in the legislative process, whether through consultative bodies, youth parliaments, or inclusion in policy design, governments can ensure that policies are reflective of and responsive to the aspirations and needs of younger generations.

Additionally, policies aimed at enhancing youth entrepreneurship and innovation can catalyze significant social and economic benefits. These include providing start-up grants, facilitating access to mentorship and venture capital, and simplifying bureaucratic processes that often hinder business creation.

Leveraging Technology for Sustainable Development

As digital natives, young people are uniquely positioned to leverage technology in the pursuit of sustainable development. This includes innovations in clean energy, sustainable agriculture, and digital healthcare solutions. Supporting youth-led technological innovation not only drives progress in these critical areas but also encourages a culture of responsibility towards the planet and future generations.

Governments, corporations, and educational institutions can support these innovations by investing in STEM education, establishing incubators and accelerators focused on sustainable ventures, and creating platforms for young innovators to showcase their solutions.

Cultural Shifts and Social Inclusion

The cultural impact of youth extends beyond technology and policy into the broader realms of social norms and practices. Young people today are more inclusive and tolerant of diversity than previous generations. They champion rights for marginalized communities, advocate for gender equality, and push for policies that reflect a more comprehensive and compassionate worldview.

Preparing for a world transformed by youth means embracing these cultural shifts and promoting inclusivity at all levels of society. This can be achieved by re-evaluating traditional narratives and structures that no longer align with contemporary values and by promoting a culture that values diversity and the benefits it brings.

Preparing for a world transformed by youth requires a multifaceted approach that includes adapting educational systems, involving young people in policymaking, supporting technological innovation, and embracing cultural shifts towards inclusivity. By doing so, societies can not only harness the immense potential of young individuals but also ensure that the world they inherit is one where they have had a hand in shaping—a world that is innovative, inclusive, and resilient. As we look ahead, it is clear that the youth of today are not just the leaders of tomorrow; they are the pioneers of a new era, ready to redefine what it means to live in a global community.

ppp

"As the world changes, so too do the roles of its young architects. Their visions for the future are foundations built on innovation, inclusivity, and an indomitable spirit of change."

ppp

TWENTY-ONE
SUMMARY

As we conclude our exploration of the vibrant and transformative impact young minds are having across various spheres of life, it becomes clear that the future is not only shaped by the dreams and actions of today's youth but also deeply dependent on their vision and energy. This book has traversed a wide landscape of themes, each demonstrating how young individuals are not waiting for permission to make their mark on the world—they are forging ahead, breaking new ground, and crafting a future that reflects their values and aspirations.

From the realm of technological innovation to environmental advocacy, and from artistic expression to social activism, young people are leading from the front. They are redefining the pathways of change, making significant strides in fields traditionally dominated by more experienced individuals, and proving that age is but a number when it comes to making a substantial impact.

Technological Innovation and Ethical Considerations

Young innovators are utilizing technology not just for the sake of innovation but with a keen focus on ethics and sustainability. They harness the power of digital tools to create solutions that address pressing global issues such as climate change, accessibility, and the democratization of education and healthcare. Their work in developing apps, platforms, and technologies reflects a deep commitment to using innovation for social good, ensuring that their creations benefit humanity and do not exacerbate existing disparities.

Environmental Advocacy and Sustainable Development

In the face of global environmental challenges, young activists are not sitting back. Instead, they are utilizing their voices and platforms to advocate for sustainable practices and policies. Through movements both local and global, they are pushing for urgent action on climate change, biodiversity loss, and pollution, making clear that environmental stewardship is not just a responsibility but a necessity for the survival of future generations.

Art and Culture as Catalysts for Change

The cultural contributions of young individuals highlight their role in using art and media to influence and educate. Through music, film, literature, and digital content, they address themes of social justice, mental health, and community solidarity. Their creative expressions serve not only as reflections of their identities and experiences but also as powerful tools for cultural diplomacy and social cohesion.

The New Face of Activism and Social Justice

Youth activism has transformed significantly, leveraging online platforms to organize, mobilize, and raise awareness. Young people are at the forefront of social justice movements, advocating for policies and practices that promote gender equality, racial equity, and economic inclusivity. Their ability to coordinate global actions quickly and efficiently exemplifies a new era of activism that is inclusive, informed, and impactful.

Education and Leadership for the Future

Recognizing the critical role of education in shaping future leaders, young people are advocating for educational reforms that include more inclusive curricula, practical learning opportunities, and access to technology. They are not only consumers of educational content but also creators, contributing to educational resources that are accessible and relevant to diverse populations.

Mentorship and the Transfer of Knowledge

The importance of mentorship in nurturing the potential of young minds cannot be overstated. Experienced mentors play crucial roles in guiding the younger generation through the complexities of their careers and personal development. This transfer of knowledge and wisdom is vital for ensuring that young individuals are well-equipped to navigate and lead in an increasingly complex world.

Resilience in the Face of Adversity

Perhaps one of the most defining characteristics of today's youth is their resilience. Despite facing global uncertainties and numerous challenges, they demonstrate an incredible capacity to adapt, persevere, and thrive. This resilience is not just beneficial for their personal growth but is also a crucial asset for societies looking to navigate the disruptions of the 21st century.

In summary, the stories and insights shared in this book provide a compelling look at how young individuals are not merely passing through this world; they are actively shaping it to reflect a more just, sustainable, and inclusive vision. Their journeys remind us that each step taken in pursuit of this vision, no matter how small, contributes to the larger narrative of change and progress.

As we look to the future, it is clear that supporting and empowering youth is not just an investment in individual futures but in the future of the world itself. The energy, creativity, and determination of young minds are invaluable resources that, if nurtured, have the potential to lead societies into a new era marked by unprecedented innovations and a deeper sense of global community. This book, therefore, serves not only as a celebration of what young people have achieved but also as a call to action for everyone—regardless of age—to support and participate in the journey toward a future shaped by the bold dreams and actions of the youth.

▷▷▷

Citation And References

This book represents the culmination of extensive research and meticulous analysis, incorporating a diverse range of sources, including numerous books, scholarly studies, and personal experiences. Additionally, I have scoured various websites to gather relevant information and data essential for the compilation of this work. I have taken every precaution to ensure the accuracy of the information presented and have diligently cited all sources to acknowledge their contributions.

Despite these efforts, the possibility of inadvertent errors remains. I deeply value the insights of my readers and appreciate any feedback that can help identify and rectify such inaccuracies. I encourage you to bring any discrepancies to my attention.

Your feedback is not only welcome but crucial, as it will aid in correcting current editions and enhancing the content of future ones. I am committed to maintaining the highest standards of accuracy and reliability in my work and thank you for your support and understanding.

Additionally, I firmly uphold the principle of freedom of speech and expression as guaranteed under Article 19(1)(a) of the Constitution of India, and I respect the diverse viewpoints and expressions of all readers.

ᐅᐅᐅ

Other Books Of The Author

1. Empowering Minds: A Journey into Women's Self-Discovery and Power
2. The Dynamics of Motivation: Catalyzing Thought into Action
3. Meditation and Mental Well Being: The Path to Inner Peace and Clarity
4. The Psychology of Child Education: Nurturing Future Generations
5. Ethical Enlightenment: A Modern Guide to Living with Integrity
6. Voices of Empowerment: Stories of Women Rising Against Odds
7. Social Psychology in Everyday Life: Understanding Human Connections
8. The Essence of Motivational Speaking: Inspiring Change in Others
9. Balancing Acts: Women, Work, and the Will to Lead
10. Guiding with Grace: Raising Children with Compassion and Awareness
11. The Power of Positive Aging: Embracing Life After Fifty
12. Building Resilient Communities: Social Work in Action
13. The Ethical Educator: Principles for Teaching and Learning
14. From Insight to Impact: Social Psychology for a Better World
15. The Ethics of Empathy: A Guide to Ethical Living
16. The Science of Empowering the Self: Navigating Life's Challenges with Psychological Wisdom
17. The Mindful Conscious Leader: Meditation Techniques for Modern Management
18. Pioneering Spirit: Women's Pathways to Leadership and Empowerment
19. Feeling to Healing: The Role of Emotional Intelligence in Child Development
20. Transformative Talks and Words of Inspiration: Insights into Motivational Oratory

ΦΦΦ

Dr. Minakshi Bansal
Social Activist
Ahmedabad, Gujarat, Bharat
minakshiindiag20@yahoo.com

❧❧❧

|| LOKAHA SAMASTHAHA SUKHINO BHAVANTU ||

• 131 •